The Strife Buster

A 30 Day Journey to Ending the Cycle of Strife

Shawn Patrick Williams D.D.

Independently Published

Kindle/Amazon

Copyright 2020
ISBN 9781698077994

Published by: HoltPublishing.Yolasite.com

Graphics & Cover Design: Vickie Holt

Shawn Patrick Williams, Author

The Strife Buster: A 30 Day Journey to Ending the Cycles of Strife

ISBN

Library of Congress Control #:

Warrior Nations Publications

PO Box 2352

Greenwood, South Carolina 29646

864-227-0508

www.warriornations.org

DEDICATION

Pastoring a small congregation for many years and specializing in Christian counseling, one of the most common problems I have found that believers have to face is the cycle of strife. Strife is destructive and a cancer to any relationship. It doesn't matter if it is your marriage, your children, your friends, or your church, strife will destroy the relationship if you don't deal with it. This book was written to help a believer understand and deal with the pattern of what I call the strife cycle.

My prayer is that you meditate on each days challenge and scripture. Apply it to your situation daily and try to see what obeying God's Word can do in your life. Take the lessons to heart and give it your best effort to see the negative effects of strife broken in your relationships.

Gathering the Harvest for the King,

Shawn Patrick Williams

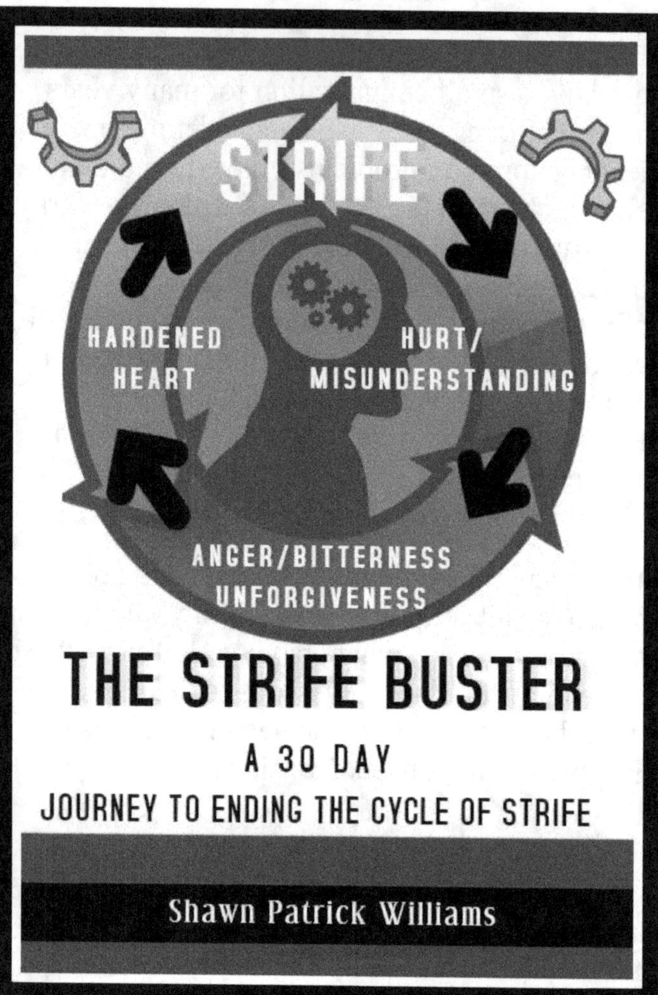

STRIFE
HARDENED HEART
HURT/ MISUNDERSTANDING
ANGER/BITTERNESS UNFORGIVENESS
THE STRIFE BUSTER
A 30 DAY
JOURNEY TO ENDING THE CYCLE OF STRIFE
Shawn Patrick Williams

TABLE OF CONTENTS

Day 1

What Does Strife Do?

From the earliest times in the Bible, all the way through the New Testament until now, we see that strife has been used as a tool of division from Satan. From the account of Abraham and Lot, Moses and the children of Israel, the Judges of Israel, King David and even the apostle Paul, all had to deal with the destructive, diving power of the cycles of strife.

"And there was strife between the herdsmen of Abram's cattle and the herdsmen of Lot's cattle."
Genesis 13:7

Strife is a controversy, quarrel, or disagreement that causes contention between two or more people and ultimately tries to divide them.

How does the strife cycle bring division into your relationships?

DAY 2

Once strife starts, its nature is to become uncontrollable. The person who starts the contention usually ends up reaping more of the negative effects of the strife cycle than they wanted. Strife is uncontrollable. It spreads like water without boundaries.

"The beginning of strife is as when one letteth out water: therefore leave from contention before it meddled with you." Proverbs17:14

Have you ever noticed how hard it is to stop striving once the cycle has started?

How does the strife cycle make you feel once it's past the point of control?

Day 3

There is a direct link to strife and pride. Pride fuels strife and strife has no end. Humbling one's self to not engage in strife before it gets to late is the key. Really take a look at what the strife is about. When you do that, I guarantee you will find pride at the root of the motive to continue in strife.

"He that is of a proud heart stirreth up strife: but het that putteth his trust in the Lord shall be made fat." Proverbs 28:25

Sow a seed of humility into the strife cycle today.

What did you see happen different as a result?

DAY 4

Strife always has to have a source! Finding the source of strife and removing it from the situation would always be the easiest way to end the strife cycle. Unfortunately, most of the time, the source of strife in a situation comes from someone we love. Most of the time, it's not as simple as removing the source of strife. In this case, instead, minister love to the strife and see why the scriptures say, "Love never fails."

"Where no wood is, the fire goeth out: so where there is no talebearer, the strife ceaseth. As coals are to burning coals, and wood to fire; so is a contentious man to kindle strife." Proverbs 26:20-21

Take a look at the source of strife in your life for one day.

What did you notice about the strife cycles?

DAY 5

When a person enjoys engaging in the strife cycle and loves the process of arguing, that's a good sign that there are other sinful areas in their heart driving the ugly drama that strife brings. Strife is only the outward manifestation of a much deeper problem.

"He loveth transgression that loveth strife." Proverbs 17:19

Can you see a link between strife and other sinful area's working in the situation?

DAY 6

There is an old phrase that says, "Fight fire with fire." The Bible says to do the exact opposite. If you try to fight fire with fire you will get burned. When I see a fire, I will withdraw myself from the heat before it burns me.

"If any man teach otherwise and consent not to the wholesome words, even the words of our Lord Jesus Christ, and to the doctrine which is according to godliness; He is proud, knowing nothing, but doting about questions and strifes of words, whereof cometh envy, strife, railing, evil murmurings, perverse disputings of men of corrupt minds, and destitute of the truth, supposing that gain is godliness: From such withdraw thyself." 1 Timothy 6:3-5

Do your words edify or tear down the people around
you?

How do you need to change the way you speak to
people?

DAY 7

There is a classic story of a man and a woman fighting on the side of the road by their broken down car in the country. A man sees the situation and stops to help the woman. As the man pulls over and gets out of the car, he walks over to the country couple. 'Sir, you don't need to speak to her like that!' Bam! Out of nowhere the woman tags the innocent, Good Samaritan in the side of the head. 'Don't you dare talk to my husband like that!' the woman yelled.

"He that passeth by, and meddelth with strife belonging not to him, is like one that taketh a dog by the ears." Proverbs 26:17

I don't know about you, but every time I've tried to grab a dog by the ears, it's tried to bite me.

Have you ever got involved in someone else's arguments?

How successful were you at resolving their problems?

DAY 8

Strife is an outward, fleshly emotional expression. It is a sign of a much deeper spiritual problem.

"For where envying and strife is, there is confusion and every evil work." James 3:16

Can you identify what cycles cause strife to rise up in your relationship?

What are they?

DAY 9

Never mistake something honorable and wise for something weak. Backing down from the strife cycle might seem like your being "weak minded" at first, but it's the first key to breaking the strife cycle.

"It is an honor for a man to cease from strife, but every fool will be meddling." Proverbs 20:3

Make a purposed effort not to engage in the strife cycle, no matter what the situation is.

How was the result different from other times that you didn't back down from the battle?

DAY 10

My Daddy always used to tell me, "Life is 10% what happens to you and 90% how you respond to it." When your anger controls your actions, you are the catalyst for the strife cycle.

"A wrathful man stirreth up strife, but he that is slow to anger appeaseth strife." Proverbs15:18

Are you slow to anger?

If not, what is the reason why you let anger control your relationships?

DAY 11

The atmosphere of strife in the camp of Israel was the heaviest burden for Moses. It was the number one reason Moses was not able to enter into the promise land. Moses was trapped in the strife cycle and he got so angry that he misrepresented God to the people of Israel.

"How can I myself alone bear your cumbrance, and your burden, and your strife?" Deuteronomy 1:12

How do you think other people in your strife cycle feel?

Are you helping stop the strife cycle, or are your actions prolonging it?

DAY 12

The number one rule of war is to know your enemy. The number two rule of war is to divide and conquer. Satan will first study you to find your weak points and then use those weak points to stir up the strife cycle. Division is the result of not breaking the strife cycle.

"...Every kingdom divided against itself is brought to desolation; and every city or house divided against itself shall not stand." Matthew 12:25

What are the areas Satan uses to stir up the strife cycle in your life?

___

Can you notice patters of division as a result of the strife cycle?

What are they?

DAY 13

The Bible puts strife right up there with murder, witchcraft, and adultery. As common and trivial as the strife cycle may seem to you, God sees it in an entirely different light. He wants to end it more than you do.

"Now the works of the flesh are manifest, which are these; adultery, fornication, uncleanness, lasciviousness, idolatry, witchcraft, hatred, variance, emulations, wrath, strife, seditions, heresies, envying, murders, drunkenness, revelings, and such like: of the which I tell you before, as I have told you in times past, that they which do such things shall not inherit the kingdom of God." Galatians 5:19-21

Did you realize the spiritual consequences of strife?

How does this influence your view of the strife cycle
and why?

DAY 14

The Bible does not mention a "spirit" of strife. To rebuke a spirit of strife would be Biblically incorrect. Strife is not a spirit, but a choice. Demonic spirits can influence an atmosphere for one to engage in the cycle, but it will ultimately be a choice to stop the strife cycle.

"Now the works of the flesh are manifest, which are these...strife...they that do such things shall not inherit the kingdom of God." Galatians 5:19-21

Do you feel like there is a demonic influence in the strife cycle? Why?

When you're in the cycle, can you see the point in which you choose to engage in the process?

DAY 15

Strife is something that is fueled. It can be driven into something large, or minimized into something smaller. It all depends on the amount of fuel that is being poured on the fire. Anger is that fuel.

"Surely as the churning of milk bringeth forth butter, and the wringing of the nose bringeth forth blood: so the forcing of wrath bringeth forth strife." Proverbs 30:33

Make a purposed effort to withdraw from any type angry comments, or angry from the strife cycle today.

What did you do differently in the situation?

What did you notice different about you?

DAY 16

While correcting my son, I used to lean down close to his face to talk. I notice that he would become aggressive in his response. No matter whom you are and what age you are, people process situations different. Giving people proper time and space can help them reduce the strife cycle in their response.

"And, ye Fathers, provoke not your children to wrath: but bring them up in the nurture and admonition of the Lord." Ephesians 6:4

Do you like to provoke people to anger?

Do you like being provoked to anger? How does it make you feel?

DAY 17

The strife cycle is a never ending cycle. Unless you replace the anger with something that is an edifying factor, the cycle will never break. Negatives fuel the cycle! In order to "Bust" the cycle, you must replace what's stirring the cycle with something that will cool it.

"If you want something different, you must do something different."

"An angry man stirreth up strife, and a furious man abounds in transgression." Proverbs 29:22

DAY 18

It is impossible to see lasting change in the strife cycle without replacing the emotional negative catalyst with a Godly response.

"Let all bitterness, and wrath, and anger, and clamor and evil speaking, be put away from you with all malice: and be ye kind to one another, tender hearted, forgiving one another, even as God, for Christ's sake forgave you." Ephesians 4:31-32

What is your negative stimulus emotion in the strife cycle?

What is the Godly response you can choose to replace it with?

DAY 19

When you are faced with the choice to respond to the strife cycle with an ungodly reaction remember, your loving response is an offering to the Lord. You are not "giving in"; you are giving an offering to Jesus.

"And walk in love, as Christ also hath loved us, and hath given himself for us as an offering and a sacrifice to God for a sweet smelling savor."
Ephesians 5:2

What part of your life is lacking in love?

How can you change it?

DAY 20

Love destroys strife every time!

"Love never fails." 1 Corinthians 13:8

Do you love without conditions?

Why?

DAY 21

You do not have to be "super spiritual" to have good discernment of character. If you want to know who someone is, take notes on what they say, and how they say it. Sooner or later, what's inside will come out.

"A good man out of the good treasure of the heart bringeth forth good things: and an evil man out of the evil treasure bringeth forth evil things. But I say unto you, that every idle word that men shall speak, they shall give an account thereof in the Day of Judgment. For by thy words thou shalt be justified, and by thy words thou shalt be condemned." Matthew 12:35-37

Take notes today and what comes out of your mouth.

What did you notice? Was it good, or evil? Was it faith, or fear?

DAY 22

The strife cycle is a "self-defense" mechanism. It will automatically start up to protect from hurt. When you are truly thinking about the other person, rather than yourself, it disarms the strife cycle.

"Let nothing be done through strife, or vain glory: but in lowliness of mind let each, esteem others better than themselves." Philippians 2:3

Who do you feel threatened by and why?

Do you see a strife pattern in that relationship?

DAY 23

It is impossible to give someone something that you don't have. If you have not received God's love for yourself, how will you give God's unconditional love to someone else?

"If a man say, I love God, and hateth his brother, he is a liar. For he that loveth not his brother whom he hath seen, how can he love God whom he hath not seen? And this commandment have we from him, that he who loveth God loveth his brother, also."
1 John 4:20-21

What is the hardest area for you to love in?

Has there been something negative in your life that has happened to you in a similar area?

Have you received God's love and healing for
yourself in this area?

DAY 24

Covering people's fault, in love, is not a normal human behavior. It's engrained in the human race to expose and capitalize on people's mistakes and weaknesses. It takes the supernatural power of the Holy Spirit to create new patterns in the strife cycle.

"And above all things have fervent charity (love) among yourselves; For charity (love) covers a multitude of sin. Use hospitality one to another without grudging." I Peter 4:8-9

Do you find it difficult to cover people in their faults and weaknesses?

Who and why?

DAY 25

I'm supposed to sow something into a relationship before I reap something. Most people expect to reap love and respect from relationships before they sow it. It doesn't work like that. When you refuse to sow love and respect into the strife cycle, it only feeds the cycle. Sowing the fruits of the Spirit in faith into the strife cycle is the key to completely breaking the cycle.

"Therefore all things whatsoever ye would that men should do to you, do ye even so to them." Matthew 7:12

Do you expect to get love before you give it? Why?

DAY 26

When you choose to replace the behavior of the strife cycle with one of the elements of Philippians 4:8, you break the strife cycle and change the outcome of your situation.

"Finally, my brethren, whatsoever things are true, whatsoever things are just, whatsoever things are pure, whatsoever things are lovely, whatsoever things are of good report: if there be any virtue, and if there be any praise, think on these things." Philippians 4:8

Make a choice today to use the concepts in Philippians 4:8 in a conflict. What happened?

DAY 27

"The enemy is in the spiritual realm, the battle field is in your mind, and the victory is in your choice."

Shawn Patrick Williams

"For thou we walk in the flesh, we do not war after the flesh. For the weapons of our warfare are not carnal, but might through God to the pulling down of strongholds, casting down imaginations and every high thing that exalteth itself against the knowledge of God and bringing into captivity every thought to the obedience of Christ." 2 Corinthians 10:3-5

Today, write down every dominating thought pattern.

What did you notice? Are you recognizing a stronghold?

DAY 28

The word "soul" in 1 Peter 2:11-12 literally means mind, thoughts, and emotions. These have a direct effect on the way we speak to others. If our thoughts are out of our control, our words will be, as well.

"Dearly beloved, I beseech you as strangers and pilgrims abstain from fleshly lust, which war against your soul. Having your conversation honest amongst the gentiles." 1 Peter 2:11-12

Do you ever notice yourself saying things, out of your mouth, before you have processed them in your mind? What type of words are they? Are they tearing down or are they building up?

DAY 29

If your mind is focused on strife and all the negative elements of the cycle, there will be no peace. If your mind is focused on the Lord and His word, there will be peace, even in the strife cycle.

"Thou wilt keep him in perfect peace whose mind is stayed on thee. Trust ye in the Lord forever: for in the Lord Je-Hovah is everlasting strength." Isaiah 26:3-4

"Where ever you focus, that will become your future." Shawn Patrick Williams

Where is your mind focused?

Do you have peace?

DAY 30

It was an August summer night in 1999. I was in Central America during the Costa Rican rainy season. I was sleeping on a couch in a missionary compound, in a small village called, "Grand Del Ora" in the Mid-Southern part of the Nation. The village had a few hundred people in it, but was strategically located in the side of the mountain rage, in which the BreBre and CaBre Indians live.

I woke up at three am to the presence of something I had never felt before. It was the supernatural power, love, and Holy fear of the Holy Spirit that I had never experienced before. I looked up outside the window and saw an electric storm streaking across the sky. As I watched this awesome natural light show, spanning from one end of the skyline to the other, I heard a voice speak to me. I would later identify this voice as the same one that spoke to me during my "Damascus Road" salvation experience. It was the voice of the Holy Spirit of Jesus Christ.

The words He spoke to me would radically alter my life. What happened that night changed my character, forever. I spent eight years of my life being a hard gangster. I beat people up professionally, cheated people, and lied to people. I was completely self-centered and self-driven, but after that night I would forever be a different man. I received revelation and an impartation of love. This is what the Lord said to me this night:

"If I created the most powerful weapon in the world, it would be a weapon that could harness the awesome power of love and inject it into the heart of the masses. It would be more powerful than all the weapons of mass destruction ever made. It would subdue the hearts of kings. Love is transcendental to life. The more you have love the more you will give love. You can't give something you don't have.

"The problem between many people is they seek to find love from others first, before they give it. You must sow before you reap. You must get love from the Source of Love first and then give it to each other. You cannot truly give something that you do not have.

"This is the reason many marriages are failing. They have unmet expectations from an imperfect human, rather than a perfect God. God alone can fill and satisfy. Love never fails! Even when love is tough, it still will not fail. Tough love is still love."

As these words burned into my heart, I wrote them down intently. I began to think on these words spoken to me on this divine summer August night. I began to realize God had already created the weapon that injected love like His. The weapon is Jesus

Christ and He was injected into us by the Holy Spirit!

"Beloved, let us love one another: for love is of God;
and everyone that loveth is born of God, and
knoweth God. He that loveth not, knoweth not God.
For God is love." 1 John 4:7-8

WHAT DOES IT MEAN TO BE "SAVED"?

"That if thou shalt confess with thy mouth the Lord Jesus, and shalt believe in thine heart that God raised him from the dead, thou shalt be saved."
Romans 10:9

The word "saved" in this verse is literally translated in Greek, sōzō, and it means to be made completely whole. If you verbally acknowledge Jesus Christ as your Lord and Savior, believe that He was raised from the dead for the forgiveness of your sins, and to give you eternal life, you can be made whole physically, mentally, and spiritually. Only believe.

A PRAYER OF SALVATION

Dear God,I believe Jesus died on the cross for my sins and was raised from the dead on the third day. I ask You to forgive me of all my sins past and present. I turn from my sins and ask Jesus Christ to come into my body, soul, and spirit. I confess Jesus Christ as my Lord and Savior and ask You to cleanse me with Your blood. I ask You, O God, to completely fill me with your Holy Spirit that I may know what it means to be "born again." I thank You for deliverance in every area of my life and I ask You these things in the name of Jesus Christ. Amen."

SHAWN PATRICK WILLIAMS

About the Author

After being radically saved from 10 years of drug and occult involvement in a bar, Shawn Patrick Williams had his own Damascus road experience. Shawn Patrick received a burning commission to evangelize the United States and the world. His style of preaching brings a revival culture to the Body of Christ.

Shawn Patrick authored several books, which have been covered by nationally broadcast TV and radio networks. He has had many of his books in stores like Books-a-Million, Family Christian Bookstores, and Parable Bookstores. Shawn Patrick passionately speaks each year through radio, TV, conferences, festivals, concerts, and churches. His personal experience of the power of the Holy Spirit, powerful deliverance from addiction and the occult, and background has aided in giving him a platform to speak to the next generation of Believers. His passion is stirring the revival-fire and seeing Christ saves lives. He has a Doctor of Divinity from Day Spring University and was ordained as a bishop in 2009. He then launched Warrior Nation Fellowship, which is an apostolic network. He is founder of the apostolic training centers called i3, which is his base in Greenwood, South Carolina.

www.ingramcontent.com/pod-product-compliance
Lightning Source LLC
Chambersburg PA
CBHW061736250726
48657CB00002B/960